# sex in the seminary

### Dating, Sex and Working for God

## Ameila Strang

ARCHWAY
PUBLISHING

Archway Publishing books may be ordered through booksellers or by contacting:

Archway Publishing
1663 Liberty Drive
Bloomington, IN 47403
www.archwaypublishing.com
844-669-3957

ISBN: 978-1-6657-1856-1 (sc)
ISBN: 978-1-6657-1855-4 (hc)
ISBN: 978-1-6657-1857-8 (e)

Library of Congress Control Number: 2022902321

Print information available on the last page.

Archway Publishing rev. date: 05/06/2022

# ~ Contents ~

# ~ Introduction ~

This book began with my experience as a single seminarian attending seminary. A seminary is a school that instructs future ministers. During my colorful years of theological study, I made friends with some of the most compassionate people who have committed their lives to "working for God" while often making daunting sacrifices in their personal lives, particularly their love lives.

I have witnessed people on their path to becoming spiritual leaders overcoming incredible obstacles while searching for love. Many have guided other singles on their spiritual journey—and all without revealing the horrors occurring in their own dating experiences. Most of my colleagues handled their personal affairs with dignity while living out their call to ministry with the highest degree of integrity, adhering to a strict moral code while embracing the "What Would Jesus Do" (WWJD) mantra. They were role-model citizens of the seminary, and many refrained from dating while attending school.

On the other hand, I did not exercise such self-discipline and restraint from "worldly" behaviors. Yet, I and many other men and women like me somehow avoided expulsion from school, implication in a salacious sex scandal, and awkward summoning to a bishop's office to explain why a reporter from Channel 7 News was trying to reach us. You get the picture.

Unlike our colleagues, we were not role-model citizens. We often did not fit into the "normal" student population on campus. We rebuked the ideology that women are not allowed to be sexual goddesses, who wore red lipstick and matching red high-heeled shoes while preaching in the pulpit on Easter Sunday.

That attitude, unorthodox in the seminary, remains a substantial part of my identity and that of many of my colleagues today. We support gay marriage and speak honestly about our struggle with alcohol and drug addiction while marching with Black Lives Matter, we openly identify as being queer and support women's reproductive rights. We are seminarians (some are Christians, and some are not) who question the church's moral authority and are unafraid to examine religion's validity.

I am a Christian, a Christian who, once upon a time, did some desperate things in the name of *love* and *lust.* And when I opened to others about my dating struggles, I found that I was not the only person on campus who struggled to find the perfect mate or was desperately trying to end a relationship with a boyfriend.

Speaking for myself, my seminary experience was bat-shit crazy. To say that I was disobedient to the rules and expectations that govern most seminaries is an understatement. I explored my sexuality and embraced my femininity while attending seminary. I had sex. I had a lot of sex in the seminary.

I confess, there were many moments during my class on the Old Testament when I wanted to stand up in the middle of the classroom and scream, "So, when you speak of Eve being seduced by the serpent in the Garden of Eden, you mean she was tempted by Adam's King Cobra, right?" But as with contemporary religion, I also understood that my study of the Christian scripture is a matter of personal interpretation.

The purpose of this book is not to alter your interpretation of biblical scripture in any way. I am merely seeking to provide the world with insight into seminarians' experiences and ordained clergy trying to find love.

For the record, this book does not tell others that sex before marriage (also known as fornication) is safe or morally right. The book is a result of my honest conviction.

Typically, you are not "getting any" from a woman of the cloth. Women who are pastors have gone to great lengths to get a master's degree in divinity at a seminary and commit themselves wholeheartedly to the "call" process. Of course, there is always an exception. I just happen to be one of them.

Now, some Bible-thumping Bible school graduate will read this book and claim that the characters are spiritual but not religious, and scandalous but not "saved." Many will say that the people had no business at all being students in a seminary.

A few men I dated while attending seminary told me that the study of religion is for pure, Godly women, and there are very few good women left in the world who still fit the profile and are worthy of the clergy collar. These are the same men who have trouble maintaining a long-term relationship and being emotionally available to women during a relationship because they have mommy issues. Assholes.

My point is seminary can be a very lonely place for single students, staff, and faculty. And sometimes, seminarians find themselves making choices they would rather not confess while standing in the pulpit. Take, for example, the inappropriate relationship I had with one of my professors.

I was a first-year student in his class. He liked to take photos of his students. He told our class that he wanted to take pictures for his scrapbook. I happily posed for several pictures with another female student during the first week of class. Our professor informed us he would share the photos with his friends. Days later, a classmate brought it to my attention that my picture was on his social media pages, and she felt that it was very inappropriate because he took the photo from the back as I stood talking with another student. I looked, and she was right; he took a picture of my ass. I immediately shrugged it off as a misplaced camera angle.

Now, I must admit that I thought my professor was very sexy; but I never imagined myself engaging in a relationship with him. Romantic relationships between faculty and students are forbidden, and the rules regarding relationships between faculty and students were crystal clear.

But somehow, the boundaries became blurred the day my boyfriend broke up with me, and I approached the professor for pastoral counseling. He listened to me attentively as I cried my eyes out while sitting in his office. He offered advice and gently held my hand as he prayed with me. He wrote his cell phone number on the back of his business card and invited me to contact him anytime I needed to talk.

A few weeks later, I called the professor because my boyfriend and I had broken up again. He invited me to his home for a counseling session. We chatted over cups of coffee about my former relationship, my seminary experience, and how I was performing in his class. We talked late into the evening. He invited me to stay for dinner. We ate and watched TV. We watched *The Simpsons*, and we laughed about how the character Marg looked a lot like the president of the seminary. He said the president and Marg wore the same wig. He continued to make references about the president and shared how he was struggling with some of the viewpoints of the administration. He invited me to stay a little longer to watch one of his favorite movies. I really did not feel like staying because I had a lot of homework to do, but I did not want to offend him, so I agreed to stay.

We turned off the television about halfway through the movie. He asked me what I thought about the president's support of the LGBTQ community and how the seminary's display of the rainbow flag around campus. "Um, I don't have a problem with it. My mom is bi. God loves everyone, right?" He frowned at me with a look of disappointment. He vehemently vented about his disdain for the president's support of the LGBTQ community and shared intimate details about the many fights he had with my dean concerning the issue. I found such intimate details about what was happening behind the scenes amongst faculty, deans, and the president to be very entertaining. He thanked me for listening to him. He expressed that he did not have many friends in the area and needed someone to talk to as much as I did. He said he was lonely and felt isolated because of his stance on members of the LGBTQ community becoming ordained clergy in the church. He reached over and rubbed my back. As someone who has been around the block a few times, I knew that was my cue to leave immediately, because things were about to heat up.

I made up an excuse about needing to finish a paper and hurried towards the front door to go home. I could feel in my gut that something was wrong, and I had crossed a line by visiting the professor's home. It seemed like it took forever to slip on my snow boots. He stood over me, making small talk about our next class and the assignment.

Just as I stood upright to put on my coat, he grabbed me by the waist, pulled me close to him, and kissed me. I pushed him away. He was a man of the cloth and my professor! I was shocked, but it felt good. It had been weeks since my boyfriend had kissed me. I stood frozen near the front door. He grabbed me by my waist again and pulled me close to him. He kissed me, and I kissed him back. He unzipped my coat and removed my scarf. After a few kisses on my neck, he simply became a man who could lay hands on unmentionable parts of my body. I spent the weekend with the professor, laying hands on each other and allowing his serpent to wander in my garden. We had sex, sipped on coffee, engaged in heated theological debates, and had more sex. We agreed to see each other again but to keep our affair a secret.

Several weeks later, I learned from a gossiping third-year student during lunch that the professor was involved with another campus student. As fate would have it, the other student he was involved with on-campus is also the student I was talking to in the photo, when he captured a picture of my ass. I pretended not to care about the rumor because I wanted to believe that I was special to him. "He likes to watch movies with his students. You know, his female students," she said. She winked at me as if she knew about our relationship. I gagged and made up an excuse to leave the table. I truly felt sick to my stomach because I knew deep down inside that she was telling the truth. I marched straight to the professor's office.

I confronted him about the rumor, and he denied it. He began explaining how the gossiping third-year student was pursuing him and said she was angry that he would not accept her invitations to have sex. I did not believe him. I knew he was lying. I knew he was lying, because she is a lesbian. Nevertheless, I continued to see him. Weeks later, rumors about the professor having sex with multiple students on campus began to flourish. I became sickened by the stories, so I ended our affair. I spoke with my academic advisor about our sexual relationship and the rumors that were going around campus. Her eyes lit up and she referred me to the president of the seminary because, she said, it was a "Title IX" situation. I had no idea what she meant by a "Title IX" situation. I assume it was a term at the seminary that I was unfamiliar with.

I met with the seminary president in her office. She listened attentively to my story. She sat stoically in a chair across from me with her fist clenched in her lap. I rambled off the details of the sexual encounters I had with the professor and expressed my concern about how the affair's end would impact my grade in his class. She stared at me intensely and, at times, covered her mouth with her hand. She began to slouch in her seat and lose her stoic composure. At times, her facial expressions and foot-tapping lead me to believe that maybe I had made a mistake by coming to her. She frowned and squinted her eyes at me. I grew worried that she was about to expel me from school. Just as I was about to tell her about the rumor, she jumped from her seat and shouted, "I have a goddamn predator on my campus!" She began pacing the floor and adjusted her "Marg Simpson" wig that appeared to have shifted slightly to the left.

I could see that she was disappointed and disgusted. She encouraged me to file a grievance. She explained that the professor's actions were an abuse of power, and the professor had taken advantage of me. Taken advantage of me? Well, I'm over thirty. The sex was consensual in my mind. Besides, our role playing as Adam and Eve was certainly enjoyable. Especially when the serpent entered the garden. Deep down inside I felt sick to my stomach. "You are a fucking Judas," I thought to myself. My inner critic was awake and active, leading me to believe that I had betrayed the professor, and he was about to be crucified because of it. Before I knew it, I had jumped to my feet to save him. "No, No, No! He did not rape me or slip a date rape drug in my Coke. It was consensual. I wanted it, too." I screamed. The President looked at me with a horrified look on her face. "Sweetie, you don't understand. Do you? I'm so sorry this has happened to you and I strongly suggest you consider filing a grievance." Grievance? She seemed to have a different opinion about the definition of "consensual sex" with a member of faculty, and it had something to do with abuse of power. At that time, I did not fully understand why she recommended that I file the grievance, because I did not understand the meaning of "abuse of power." I was confused. However, I agreed to file a grievance, because I trusted her judgement. She moved about the room in a state of panic. There was a sense of urgency when the president called her secretary and requested that she immediately bring a grievance form to her office. I did not know what to write on the form. I did not fully understand what the grievance was about, so I simply wrote, "I had sex with Dr. X." The President assured me that they would be in contact with me shortly. The administration moved swiftly to begin their investigation.

After what seemed like a *CSI: Seminary* probe into my personal life and my affair with the professor, I found myself sitting at the end of a long table in a conference room with the investigation committee. They asked me all sorts of questions about the relationship I had with my professor and my experience in the classroom. But the most embarrassing question came from the systematic theology professor, who asked, "So, what would the professor say to you after he had sex with you?" I stared back at him in disbelief from my end of the table and answered, "For the record, he said that it was the best pussy he ever had." Next question, please.

The seminary fired the professor at the end of the school year. Multiple students had filed grievances against the professor for sexual harassment prior to our encounter. However, he was given many chances to correct his behavior and failed to do so. I sought counseling immediately after the ordeal, and a therapist explained the meaning of abuse of power related to the power dynamics of faculty dating and students. According to my professor's latest post on social media, he is now a pastor at a church and is adjunct faculty at another seminary. My story is just one of thousands of stories that fortunately did not end up in the media. Though this topic or related ones may have been floating around in the media for quite some time, many still lack some especially important knowledge on this issue. Most people go on living completely unbothered by the details of the private lives of seminarians until there is a sex scandal within their congregation or a local priest is dragged away in handcuffs on the news for sexual misconduct.

Searching for a book to explain to me how to navigate the pathway between my bedroom and the pulpit wasn't at the top of the course booklist during my check-in process when I entered seminary. I wasn't prepared for the topic of sexuality to take center stage as I was studying theology.

"Is there an ethics class for dating and sex?" or "Is celibacy required for ordination?" were questions on my mind at the time, but I was too ashamed to ask my pastor before entering seminary. New student orientation did not seem like the appropriate time or place either. When I was completing my application to enter seminary, having a conversation with the admissions interview committee about sex was not on my To Do List. I was entering seminary to learn about theology, church history, how to lead a worship service, whether rye bread or whole-wheat bread was appropriate for communion, and how to lead a congregation.

No one informed me that the process of becoming a minister requires seminarians to examine their own struggles—be it with dating, sexual orientation gender identity, sexual behavior, and a host of other related concerns that are often used to define pastoral conduct. The delicate topic of sex and dating was something I didn't know how to discuss among student groups, professors, and school administrators, or at Bible study.

The fact that I was a single mom who entered seminary with two kids out of wedlock with two different baby daddies (it's a long story) pretty much told the admissions department that I was no stranger to engaging in sexual relations, and practicing celibacy wasn't a part of my personal history.

Like many seminarians, I came to seminary fresh from the church pew. Most seminarians come straight from college soon after completion of their undergraduate studies to seminary. Some date. Some party. Some have casual sex partners. Some are celibate. Some classmates wake up next to each other after a hard night of the "Jesus and A Beer" ministry at a local pub. They talk about it amongst themselves. But they do not talk about it publicly—until now.

Seminarians experience the same awkwardness of running into a bad date at the mall or even worse, at church. Where do seminarians talk openly about their own sex lives? Most often, in their diaries. It can be difficult for seminarians to share the intimate details of their personal lives, especially when the church has embraced that a "don't ask, don't tell" policy is best for the seminary and the congregation.

On the following pages of this book, you will find a zany chronicle of a collection of kind-of –sort-of true dating stories "inspired" by the real-life dating seminarians who have shared their stories with me over the years during lunch, by stories I acquired simply eavesdropping on conversations in the library, and by my own personal dating stories. These stories are shared as diary entries. The diary entries are an ode to the dating experiences, intimacy, and sex. The names of the seminarians have been changed to protect those who are leading congregations today.

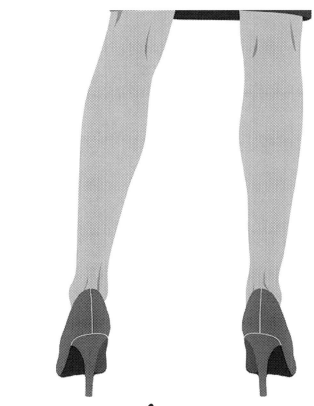

# Sex in the Seminary

# Bust the Windows Out Your Car

Dear Diary,

He betrayed me again. Now there is no guarantee at this point that Ben won't find his pet bunny boiling in a pot when he comes home from work, like the cheating husband in the movie *Fatal Attraction*, but I can't make any promises. I don't know what emotion is more powerful inside of me right now. I feel rage, shame, sadness, and guilt, and watching television shows such as *Snapped*, *Women Who Kill*, or *The First 48* isn't helping my mood either. Truthfully, I think I've gone mad. OK, I've gone batshit insane. I've always been a levelheaded, composed, and dignified woman. But this man, this boy, Ben, has taken my emotions to a place I thought they would ever escalate to.

I will merely state there are four reasons why strongly suggesting that taking a sledgehammer to his car is not such a bad idea. If I had a sledgehammer right now, I would smash his car up until it's unrecognizable. That Mustang would be nothing but a slab of chrome. I know that vengeance is the Lord's, so I will take a chill pill for the moment.

How could Ben do this to me? How could he cheat on me? I'm feeling all sorts of emotions over this sorry excuse for a man. I want to cry, but I'm so upset that the tears evaporate in my tear ducts. Three years! Three years devoted to him, for him to do this to me.

The other woman is also a seminarian. If you ask me, she is the bitchiest person at the school.

He broke up with me because he was tired of my "rejection" when he attempted to initiate sex. I never rejected him. I was hesitant most of the time when he asked me to have sex with him. Don't get me wrong. I know that sex is essential in a relationship, and it is important for my partner to feel desired, but I told him upfront when we started dating how I felt about premarital sex.

I tried to explain to him that I grew up in a very conservative Christian home. My mom never discussed sex with me. She only told me that premarital sex is a sin and I should not do it. My mother was also a preacher, and I remember how she used to stand at the pulpit of our church and preach about the negative consequences of having sex outside of wedlock. I'm talking "fire and brimstone" messages that evoked an intense fear in me and probably most of the sexually active members of the congregation. She would talk about sexually transmitted diseases, AIDS, and unwanted pregnancies. If we lived in an earlier time, I'm pretty sure she would've had me in a titanium chastity belt on my twelfth birthday.

The thought of burning in hell for having sex before marriage didn't agree with my hormones and burning sensual desires. The fear didn't keep me from having sex. However, after having sex for the first time, I felt so much shame. Still, I couldn't understand how something that felt so good could be so contemptible.

Oh, how I loved being in a relationship with Ben. Sex was the only real issue. He acts like I never gave in to his advances. I'll admit we didn't have sex often. However, considering my feelings on the matter and the internal turmoil I had to suppress each time, one would think my love in other areas would've more than compensated for the times I told him, "Not tonight, baby," or "I can't, my love. I have a splitting headache."

Many nights, I would lie in bed thinking of how I could not live up to the morals and values my mom instilled in me, rather than how much I loved the man I was intimate with. I couldn't enjoy the moment and absolutely couldn't enjoy the moments afterward. Three years with this jerk, and it ends like this?

Was the lack of sex good enough reason for him to sleep with another woman? And did it have to be a woman who attended the same school as us? I mean, this seems so unfair.

We had numerous talks about marriage. We went to open houses in hopes of finding our first home together. Now he's willing to throw all of what we shared away because I wouldn't share my body with him at his beck and call. How can I deal with all this emotional damage and guilt? Ben should be punished for his careless handling of my heart, and all over sex.

I wonder if the boyfriends of the other women here at the seminary cheat. Maybe there's a coalition of undersexed guys dating women of the clergy who take an oath to be unfaithful. I'm still contemplating going to the hardware store and picking up a sledgehammer.

*–Seminarian 1*

# Great Sex, Babe, But Does He Have to Watch?

*Dear Diary,*

*There was a time when I thought dating women* at the seminary was my best option for finding women with whom I could be equally yoked. I was delusional. The women here are too conservative and uptight. One thing I can't stand is a prudish woman.

Most of the women here are feminists who are too self-righteous for my temperament. They are always on edge and can't take a compliment. Seriously, what's wrong with telling a beautiful woman that she looks sexy in a dress? Can't a God-fearing man say to a child of God she'll have more sex appeal if she wore lip gloss and a little freaking eye shadow without it being abhorrent? I've had about all I can take with these seminarian women. I've pretty much blacklisted every one of them. Yes, indeed, I'm done.

I started looking outside of the seminary for women I could share my love with. In fact, I started dating one girl off campus who says she's "spiritual" but nonreligious. It's not the ideal match, but I took a liking to her rather quickly. The way she described her faith and spirituality immediately brought to mind some New Age cult-type stuff. I don't judge. So, it wasn't a deal breaker. But things got a little strange after our first date.

For our second date, Tonya invited me over to her place for dinner. When I entered the house, the first thing I noticed were some crystals on her fireplace. I did not ask any questions, and she didn't tell me right away that she believe the crystals had healing powers. So, I assumed they were just decorations or something. But when I discovered more crystals sitting around her bed, I had to ask what was going on.

She told me the crystals kept her chakras balanced, and she made her entire apartment a sanctuary. I guess it's possible for a person to love crystals that much, but something told me there was more.

I casually peaked into her bedroom and saw a picture of an old man hanging over her bed. I asked Tonya who he was, and she told me it was her deceased grandfather. It didn't bother me that she had a picture of her grandfather in her room, and after listening to her stories about how he was a Southern Baptist minister and how her grandparents raised her in the church, I understood how much she adored him. However, it felt awkward trying to be intimate with her in her bedroom. Lying in bed with her just felt weird. It felt like he was watching us and critiquing my lovemaking skills. I'd look up at various moments while we were doing our thing, and his messianic pose and pious eyes seemed fixated on me—following the movements of my body with each stroke. When I say it was weird, I mean it was the creepiest sex I've ever had.

Having sex with Tonya was phenomenal, aside from the quiet voyeur staring at us. I thought it was a personal issue that I had to deal with. So, I didn't say anything to her, like asking her to turn the pictures around or remove the crystals from around her bed.

We saw each other for a few more dates. One day she disclosed that the universe gave her healing powers. I didn't overthink it. We put in six months of dating, fantastic sex, and her nonreligious ways. The truth of the matter is that good sex could make the strangest relationship tolerable. So I thought. The day she told me about her healing powers, I should have run for the hills. Despite our different beliefs in higher power sources within the universe, I decided to hang around.

One day, I was sick with a cold. Why did I tell Tonya that? There was a bunch of herbs and stuff she offered to rub on my body. I laid on her bed naked, covered from head to toe in a white, floral-scented paste with her grandfather staring, piously down at me from the wall. Tonya was confident that her home remedy would heal my body. When she wasn't looking, I tiptoed across the room, reached into my duffle bag and took two doses of cold and flu medicine. Hours later, I started to feel better, but I allowed her to believe it was through the powers bestowed upon her. I felt there was no reason to hurt someone's feelings over something so trivial.

Tonya was such a sweet girl. Her devotion to her spirituality was admirable. She also had a body equivalent to a non-surgically enhanced, natural version of Kim Kardashian, and she knew how to please a man. All good reasons to stay.

But after six months, enough was enough.

I had had it with having sex and the permanent gaze and imagined judgments about my performance from her grandfather in the picture. I was over her natural healing remedies and entertaining a constant feeling she would eventually try to persuade me to join some cult. That experience with Tonya was enough to drive me back to dating the women on campus. Big sigh. Yup. It's back to swimming in the pool with all those middle-of-the-road, unprogressive, uptight seminary sharks.

*—Seminarian 2*

# The Quickest Date in the Guinness Book of Records

Dear Diary,

I met this gorgeous man the other day. Howard was his name. We started following each other on social media immediately. It wasn't long before we were in each other's DMs. I was quick to accept his invitation to have dinner with him at the best Italian restaurant in town.

I put on my best outfit, which my frame filled in all the right places. I felt like an A-list celebrity as Howard escorted me into the establishment. He confirmed our reservations with the hostess, and as she took us to our table, I was in complete awe as I took in the restaurant's enchanting interior design.

Feeling myself and all of my femininity, I was charmed by his gentlemanly gesture of pulling out the chair before he took his seat at the table. The waiter came and took our drink orders. He had already told me about their best dish. So, we gave her our entrée orders as well.

I was glad to see him in person again, not that I didn't enjoy looking at him modeling in all his pictures on the 'Gram. There we were together in the flesh. No emoji could replace the ear-to-ear grin on my face as we had a pleasant conversation while waiting for our food. Casually, he asked about my vocation. I cleared my throat and began nervously tapping my foot under the table. I'm proud of my choice to answer God's calling for me to be a shepherd for His people, but I loathe having to answer that question.

It could be a deal-breaker for many men. I reluctantly told him that I was a seminary student preparing to become a pastor. He didn't probe, and I felt he was unnerved by my confession. About an hour later, I excused myself to go to the restroom. Relieved, I remember thinking to myself that Howard had some real boyfriend potential as I walked to the ladies' room. When I returned to our table, he was gone. My first thought was that he went to the restroom also. After fifteen minutes, it became clear to me that he wasn't in the men's room.

I walked outside to see if he was smoking or having an important phone call. He wasn't out there. I looked around the parking lot. I didn't remember where he parked, but even so, there was no sign of him. At this point, I wasn't ready to accept that he was gone. I went back into the restaurant and scanned all the tables.

I saw our waiter signal for me come to the table because he was ready to serve us. Accepting my denial, I silently went into shock as I faced reality. I walked back to the table and thanked the waiter as he placed our food on the table. I wanted to cry. I felt my eyes tearing, but I held my composure.

I sat at the table with two plates of Chicken Alfredo and a basket of buttery biscuits that Im sure was delicious, but the embarrassment of my date sneaking out while I was in the restroom took away my appetite and impaired my tastebuds. I chewed for show. I wonder what his exit strategy would have been if I hadn't excused myself from the table. Howard was a coward, but so was I. Mortified by the experience, I never told the waiter to remove the second plate. I just sat quietly nibbling on the biscuits. Although I'm sure he figured it out when he brought the bill, and a dismal party of one paid for a dinner meant for two.

*—Seminarian 3*

# If Only Jesus Were My Loverboy Valentine

Dear Diary,

For Valentine's Day, I posted the following message on social media: "Jesus is my Valentine." Not! OMG, I cannot believe I wrote that crap! I'm so full of shit. Who am I kidding? My friends must think I have lost my mind. Maybe I have. To even toy with the notion of dating Jesus and then going as far as changing my status on Facebook to "in a relationship" would get me committed to an institution for sure. It's pathetically humorous when I think about it.

Of course, I'm exaggerating a bit. Cupid has made a drive-by in my love life a few times after the bitterly contentious divorce from my ex-husband. Still, that little blonde, winged infant-god must be dipping his arrow tips in a diluted love potion these days, because I'm still hemorrhaging from the atrocious last date I had.

Part of me feels a little guilty, giving so much attention to romance, or the lack thereof, instead of giving all of me to a transcendent relationship with God. After all, I'm going to be a pastor one day. But I don't like these endless nights of sleepless solitude. It's unbearable.

Being single these days is so trying. I lay in bed night after night, berating myself. My love for Jesus should be enough, shouldnt it? What mortal man could compare to the son of God? No matter how many times I try to convince myself that not all men are scrubs or dogs, and how patience is a virtue, I'm always met with stubborn opposition internally.

These yearnings are intense and worrisome. I grapple and toss restlessly in my mind about whether dating is an unnecessary distraction preventing me from focusing on my studies. I find myself asking, what example will I set for the single members of my future congregation? How will I counsel them if I feel this way about myself and discontented with my own love life?

*—Seminarian 4*

# Still Making Babies at Sixty

Dear Diary,

I ran into a dear friend I hadn't seen in a while on campus today. I hadn't seen Nancy for a few months. She's a 60-year-old seminarian working towards her doctoral degree. She is one of the sweetest people I've ever met in or outside of the seminary.

I saw her first from a distance, and I could tell something was wrong with her. Nancy always wore one of the loveliest smiles, but today it seemed like something had drained all the joy from her body. I waved to her, but she didn't see me. Her mouth was downturned, and her body posture bent as if buckets of water were in each hand and weighing her down. As I got closer, I could see more clearly the pained expression on her face. She was oblivious to her surroundings because she still didn't seem to notice my presence—not even when I called her name within earshot.

I put my hand on her arm, and she flinched slightly. Once she recognized that it was me, she forced a cordial smile. I asked her if everything was okay. She let her hands fall to her side. As she drew in her shoulders, a heavy sigh escaped from her mouth. I suggested to her that we sit down. We walked to a nearby bench and sat down. She immediately covered her face with her hands and burst into tears. I'd never seen Nancy this way. I didn't pressure her to speak, but I did assure her that I was there to listen if she chose to share.

After several moments, her sobs began to taper, and she lifted her chin to look at me with a gracious sparkle in her eyes. The last time I saw Nancy, she and her boyfriend had broken up. I handed her a tissue from my handbag. After blowing her nose and clearing her throat, she told me that she and her ex had started talking again. She went on to say that things have escalated, and they were rekindling old passions. Nancy said they've had sex on more than one occasion. I remember thinking to myself how I hope my sex life is still fiery when I get to be her age.

What shocked me was not her matured libido or that they had unprotected sex. When she told me, she thought she might be pregnant, my eyes got wide, and for a few seconds, I forgot how to breathe. I can't make this shit up. Really, I can't.

*–Seminarian 4*

# Hmmm… Should I Pose Wearing My White Clergy Collar or My White Lingerie?

*Dear Diary,*

*I let my inner freak out today. I needed some* "Vitamin D" badly—the kind of nourishment you can't get from the sun. I uploaded new profile pics, and they did precisely what I hoped they would—get attention. Ask, and you shall receive. Never have more real words been written.

I can be just as superficial as any other person, but I know how to spot a person's essence with clothes on or off. My current wasteland of romance and lust goes to show that female pastors are neither desired nor pursued by men—at least not the men in the world of online dating. My sexuality is a gift from God, but it seems the work I do for God negates all my sensuous allure.

*—Seminarian 5*

# New Week, Another New Man

Dear Diary,

I've been so busy lately, out and about in these streets living my best life as a happily single woman. I called things off with Greg. Ordinarily, I don't have many regrets in life about anything I do, but having my boyfriend come to the church I'm interning at was perhaps the most foolish thing I've ever done.

Don't get me wrong. It was nice having him at Bible study from time to time. His presence occupying one of the seats on the sanctuary's back row the Sunday mornings when it was my turn to preach was the pleasant support that I felt I needed. I wish the parishioners and members of the church had not developed a fondness for him. It's not surprising, considering how charismatic Greg is.

He and I were together for three years. I thought what we had was solid. So, the thought of a public breakup never crossed my mind. About three weeks ago, Greg instigated an argument in the church's parking lot. How embarrassing! The same way I wouldn't go to anybody's place of employment and start a fight in front of their co-workers, I hoped my personal affairs wouldn't leak into the whispered gossip of the church members where I'm interning. That parking lot tiff wasn't the only reason I broke up with him, but it was another event I could group with the other instances which had already started the downward spiraling of our relationship.

I thought that returning to the dating scene again after being off the market for three years of monogamy would be difficult. I haven't forgotten the games people play, but I fell back into the role of independent, single lady like a pro. At the moment, I'm dating two men. You would think I would refrain from bringing men to the church, but I invited one of them to join me for service two weeks ago and another one of my suitors the following week.

Everyone has gotten used to seeing Greg there. I can only imagine what the parishioners are thinking now that Greg has vanished. I can tell they don't quite know what to make of his disappearing act. When Greg stopped showing up for events, people took notice, just as I'm sure people have observed how new performers are now playing the same role he had. No one has dared to ask me directly, but that hasn't stopped them from speculating about it.

When Greg first started attending services, I introduced him as my "special guest." With time, it became more evident who he was to me. It must've come as a shock to see me arriving with two different male special guests in less than a month, especially so soon after Greg and I had such an explosive argument on the church grounds. I guess I should use more discretion with my "special guests," especially since they are always men. I've never brought any women to the church as a special guest, except for my mom. She's special, but I introduced her as my mother.

*—Seminarian 5*

# I Heard You, But I Wasn't Listening

Dear Diary,

I don't know why but I've always had a problem listening. As a child, my parents had my hearing examined. It was after one of my teachers reported that I often failed to respond to her calling my name in class. You can't imagine how embarrassing it was for me when the teacher would ask me to repeat the last thing spoken, and I couldn't even pretend that I had a clue.

It was difficult for me to understand the words spoken to me. I would get confused in conversations. What's interesting is that, according to the audiologist, I did very well on the hearing test. He couldn't find a cause for the issue. He even gave me a gold star sticker.

Needless to say, as a grown woman, I still have trouble understanding people when they speak to me. When dating and trying to get to know someone through the exchange of stories, thoughts, and expressed feelings, listening is critical to building a foundation for the relationship based on effective communication.

My inadequate listening skills was the catapult to my breakup with Justin on Saturday. The last attempt we made to be physically intimate was a disappointment because he couldn't get an erection. Naturally, I asked him if it was me. He denied it and said that his oxytocin level probably was low. Oxytocin is a hormone that plays a part in sexual activity. It's one of the reasons people call it the "love hormone." Well, I mistakenly thought he said OxyContin.

Even though I heard wrong, when I heard him say that my mind immediately went to my former roommate. She struggled with opioid addiction for years. Her whole family got behind her and had an intervention to get her proper help.

I felt as if I knew exactly what to do. This was my man, and if we couldn't enjoy sex because he was making destructive lifestyle choices, I was bent on assisting him in getting help. I didn't want to have a conversation about his addiction until I had gathered some information. Once I had a chance to research how Oxycontin abuse could cause sexual dysfunction in men, I invited him to dinner at my place so we could chat.

When I felt the time was right, I brought up my concerns. I was a little nervous, which made me talk fast, and because I cared so much for him, my emotions got the best of me. As I spoke, my hands floundered, and I left no space in my monologue for Justin to interrupt me. I gave him the articles I printed from the internet, along with a list of names for support groups and rehab facilities that could help him on a journey to recovery. I opened up about my Aunt Pat, which I hadn't done with anyone outside of my family. I told Justin about her triumph over the use of controlled substances. I assured him I would be in his corner every step of the way.

Then, as my eyes narrowed and my eyebrows pulled down in concentration, I soothed the tone of my voice most sympathetically as I offered to pray for him. I stopped speaking. Sighing deeply, I noticed for the first time that, except for his squished eyebrows, Justin had somewhat of a lack of expression on his face. His eyes blinked rapidly, and as I leaned in closer to pat him on the leg, his facial expression began to show disgust.

Justin said sharply, "I don't have a drug problem. I've never done drugs in my life." I just knew he was in denial. After clarifying that he said oxytocin and not OxyContin, he quickly gathered his things to leave and told me not to call him again as he shut the door behind him.

I had made a complete fool of myself. I had never felt so embarrassed in my life. Now I'm wondering if I heard God's call to the ministry correctly. The seminary is helping me to help others and save lives. But if I can't hear what people say, I run the risk of insulting more innocent people and making matters worse instead of better.

*—Seminarian 6*

# What He Doesn't Know Hurts Me More Than Him

*Dear Diary,*

*Last night, I hooked up with this guy named* Adonis. I don't know if his parents named him that or if dozens of women had created the nickname for him. Wherever he got the name, it was fitting. He was indeed a very handsome young man. The date had all the makings for being a good one. We got pizza from this authentic brick oven pizzeria not too far from the seminary. We walked along the pier and talked for a couple of hours, laughing and flirting underneath the stars. It started getting late, and I didn't want the date to end. I gave all the feminine, coquettish nonverbal signals I could, so he knew I wanted more than a kiss to end the night. He caught each cue and sent a few of his own that turned me on. He couldn't afford to pay for a hotel room. So, I suggested a place that I knew. He wasn't familiar with the school or the area. I didn't purposely choose not to tell him it was on my seminary campus, but I didn't.

There was a dormitory building deep on the school grounds that was under construction. Adonis thought it was a hot idea. We decided to go and arrived there within a few minutes. It was a perfect spot for us to unleash our animalistic, raw cravings.

The heat consumed us. The thought of getting caught by campus security didn't frighten us but thinking of the possibility intensified the excitement. It was the hottest sex I'd ever had.

When we were done and fixing our clothes, he asked how I knew about this place. I thought I had already told him I was a student there. So, I reminded" him, and he seemed not the least bit stunned or turned off. There was no uncomfortable energy or awkward body language. I figured he remembered me telling him, which is why it wasn't breaking news or anything alarming.

Well, fast forward to today. I called him three times, and each time I got no answer. A few minutes ago, I decided to text him, and he replied almost instantly with a message using all caps that said I should've told him I was seminarian before we had sex and that he never wanted to see me again. Never was it more clear to me that life as a shepherd to God's people came at a high cost. Nothing left to say but, *Damn!*

*—Seminarian 6*

# Since I'm Trying Tantric Sex for You, Can You Try Shutting Up for Me?

Dear Diary,

I bumped into Mashala today when I was in the seminary's campus library. The self-proclaimed "yogi" didn't see me. Thank heaven for that. But I must say, she still looks as fine as she did when we were having our little fling. I felt tempted to approach her, but that was penis encouraging me. My brain, on the other hand, strongly protested and immediately remembered why we stopped fooling around—most importantly, why we stopped talking to one another altogether.

We only went on one date but had sex four times that same night. We spoke a few times on campus before actually setting up a plan to go out. I knew she was Unitarian, but I didn't know too much about her until we were on our date and had an opportunity to chat. I was quick to learn that she would take any chance she could to speak. She liked talking… a lot.

I have ADHD, so listening to her talk incessantly was challenging, because it wasn't long before I ceased hearing words; they became irksome chatter. However, my ears pinged when I heard her say, "tantric sex." She had my full attention.

I didn't know anything about it. As long as it didn't require talking, I was all in. I think she said it is a Hindu or Buddhist thing. I found it interesting how her talkativeness became less of an annoyance to me while I listened to her explain how during tantric sex, the aim was to be present at the moment of sexual fulfillment by exploring your partner's body and being more aware of your own.

She didn't have to try hard to persuade me. As gorgeous as Mashala was, tantric sex sounded like it could probably cure my ADHD.

I couldn't wait to see her naked. I was a quick learner and managed to master the different positions quickly. The sex was unique and fun. It was the best sex I had had in years. Not only was it enjoyable, but I found it therapeutic. Goodbye, Adderall.

I eventually fell asleep. When I woke up, she was talking about her Biblical interpretations of premarital sex. I couldn't take her rambling anymore. She was a beautiful girl, and I'll forever be grateful to her for introducing me to tantric sex. But she talked too much. I told her I had schoolwork to do, got dressed and got the heck out there.

She called the next day, but I didn't answer, and I never called her following that night. Still, it was nice to see her at the library today. One thing's for sure, if I do hook up with her again, I'll make sure to have at least have a muzzle.

*—Seminarian 7*

# This Closet Isn't All that Bad, So I Don't Think I'll Come Out... Ever!

Dear Diary,

Eric is back in town. He called me the other day and asked if I wanted to meet him for drinks. Of course, I said yes. He was the first guy I slept with and the only other person who knows I'm gay. The seminary unapologetically supports members of the LGBTQ+ community becoming clergy. Still, I don't want to disclose my sexual orientation with anyone there officially.

When Eric and I got together, it was like no time had passed. He is still as cute as ever, and with a few drinks in him, seductive as hell. The heat that rose between us that night came to a climax of unbridled, reinvigorated sexual desire.

Now, I'm left asking myself, "Why did we sleep together?" He wants a relationship. Part of me wants the same thing, I guess. I know that I wouldn't be able to handle sex buddies or friends-with-benefits type of arrangements, so a relationship seems logical. I care for him, but committing to him in the romantic sense would eventually mean introducing him to my family.

No way am I ready to come out to my parents, especially my dad. He's a pastor with strong opposition to homosexuality. I've successfully managed to hide my sexuality all my life. I've gotten good at deception for the sake of protection. My first time with Eric was under my parents' noses when I was living with them.

I don't want to hurt my father, and I know starting a serious relationship with Eric would be devastating for him. I don't know which would be the worst for him. Believing that your only son is an abomination damned to roam the pits of hell for being gay, or having the congregation you've been called to guide and counsel ceasing to respect you because of your gay seminarian son.

My dad was so proud when I told him about my acceptance into the seminary. He couldn't wait to let the bishop and his colleagues know about me starting school in the fall. Eric comes from a nonreligious family. They welcomed his homosexuality without abhorrence. He couldn't understand why I needed approval from my dad when I already had God's blessing plus the support of the seminary. The risk is too high that I'll lose my family. One day I might open the closet door and come out. It pains me, but I won't expect Eric to wait.

*—Seminarian 8*

# Even with a Mental Illness, Don't I Deserve a Chance at Romance?

Dear Diary,

I can't explain how much Timothy means to me. He's everything I've ever hoped for and more. His kindness has no limits, and I'm grateful for his support while I juggle a demanding class schedule at the seminary. He's a seminarian also. So, he can empathize with how stressful it can be, and we share similar career goals. Sometimes, I'm not sure if he is real. He seems too good to be true, and I start to worry that I may have lost touch with reality and am merely imagining he exists.

Psychosis isn't a symptom for every person with a diagnosis of bipolar, but it's possible. My mom is the only person who knows of my diagnosis. I'm afraid to tell Timothy about it. I fear that disclosing it to him would beckon the Grim Reaper to come and slaughter our relationship—a relationship that I desperately want to continue nurturing and building.

Just the other day, he and I had a profound conversation. We share much of the same beliefs and have been through similar experiences in life. I thought I was dreaming as we talked, because it was the unlikeliest engagement of spiritual and emotional intimacy I've ever had with another person. I wanted to call my mom and put him on the phone so I could confirm with a "normal" person I was not hallucinating and that Timothy truly existed.

He's been impressively patient so far with my erratic mood swings, but I'm sure he's had at least one moment of suspicion that I may have a screw or two loose. He hasn't vocalized a curiosity, but all it will take is the wrong day to have the wrong episode, and then poof! My budding relationship with Prince Charming could vanish into smoke.

More than therapy, more than mood stabilizers or antipsychotics, more than support groups, but like Aretha Franklin used to sing, Timothy makes me feel like a natural or, should I say, "normal" woman. I feel safe in his arms. I feel like love is possible because I've found someone who is possibly "the one."

The other day my greatest fear manifested, and he asked if there was something wrong with me. He was very delicate the way he asked, but I could tell the jig was up. We've never discussed anything related to mental illness before. So, I didn't have any evidence to support any of the thoughts I had that Timothy fed into the dominating stigma suffocating mental health progression and awareness. He's seen me up and down. He's been compassionate and understanding of so much already. Still, I was mortified that the moment had come when I could come clean and confess my affliction.

I panicked and told him nothing's wrong—just a female hormonal thing. Dating a woman who struggles with a mental illness requires dedication and acceptance of two distinct entities, because even though I have a bipolar diagnosis, I am not my disorder. It is not my identity, but it is a part of me.

My mother doesn't see me outside of my illness. In fact, she believes I'm paying penance for childhood disobedience. I pray I don't scare Timothy away with my outburst and antics, I'll eventually muster up the courage to tell him.

*—Seminarian 9*

# I Didn't Mean to Turn You On

Dear Diary,

I don't want to get anybody fired, but I don't feel safe at the seminary anymore. The new campus maintenance man is stalking me. I don't even know the man's name. I remember seeing him my first week in the dorm and saying to myself that even with his dirty overalls and mop bucket, he was kind of cute. Our eyes met, and I smiled at him. That was it. I didn't give him any encouragement or indication that I wanted to know him personally.

After that brief, innocent exchange of friendly smiles, I started seeing him all over campus. I didn't think too much of it. After all, he is the maintenance man. It's essentially his job to have a ubiquitous presence on campus. I shrugged it off as being coincidental that he seemed to be everywhere I was. That is, until last week.

I was headed to my apartment, and he was there lurking near

my door with that filthy bucket of his. I was cordial and said, "Hello." Out of nowhere, he asked if he could take me out. I politely declined and proceeded to enter my apartment. Then, things got crazy between us. I do not know what I did to make him angry. I didn't think turning someone down for a date would lead to the degree of harassment that followed.

The first incident was when he reported to the seminary that I had bed bugs in my apartment. I guess he told the administration I had spoken to him about the bedbugs. Nevertheless, the seminary paid for pest control to inspect my apartment. Of course, they found nothing. Then, two days later, he entered my apartment when I was not home.

I returned home from work, and there was a maintenance ticket in my kitchen to fix my garbage disposal. That freaked me out. That's a home invasion! The thought of someone in my home, in my sanctuary, without consent caused a surge of apprehension to circulate throughout my body. I crept around the apartment to make sure I was alone.

I returned to the kitchen and tested the disposal for possible tampering because it worked perfectly fine when I left home that morning. What if he went into my bedroom and sniffed or stole some of my panties? Masturbated on my pillows? Installed hidden cameras everywhere? I'm so paranoid. Lord, protect me.

*—Seminarian 10*

# Let Me Introduce You to My Grandson. He's Hot!

Dear Diary,

If there's one thing I can't stand about being single, it's when people try to fix me up with someone. It happens all the time from relatives, friends, and even members of my congregation. Firstly, I don't understand why these unofficial matchmakers think I can't find a man on my own. Secondly, how can anyone, like some church members, who haven't held a single conversation with me—one that went deeper than salutations and reciprocal well-wishes to have a good day—know what values and attributes I'm looking for?

Well, this morning when I got to my office, there was a note and a photo on my desk. It was from a retired teacher who only comes to the church on the Sundays we have communion. The message had his contact information and a photo of the teacher standing beside a man with his arm over her shoulders. In addition to the phone number, name, and email address was a message that read, "I heard you were looking. Call my grandson. Isn't he hot?" I shook my head in disbelief that I held a note from a grandmother practically pimping out her grandson to her pastor. I couldn't help but burst out in laughter.

The teacher was more passive with her attempt to fix me up than others have been. So, I didn't mind too much. How could I be mad at that? Besides, he was very hot, indeed.

*–Seminarian 11*

# Attention Single Ministers Everywhere! Never Date a Parishioner

Dear Diary,

It's been six months, and Natalie still hasn't gotten over our breakup. As a seminarian, I should've known better than to get involved with a church member where I was interning. She bamboozled me. She's like the supervillain, Two-Face, in the Batman comics. She led me to believe that she was this sweet, gentle, and pretty young thing. She always had solo performances with the choir. Her voice was heavenly. Natalie seemed to be a perfect fit for a young seminarian like me. However, her flip side wasted hardly any time in revealing itself.

Our first date should have been a red flag. We were in a restaurant and she complained in a very loud and flamboyant manner to our waiter and the manager that her glass had lipstick on the brim. I don't know if she really didn't realize it was her lipstick on the cup or if she was trying to get a free meal. I should have run like a wild stallion from her gravitational pull that I didn't know then was imperceptibly sucking me deep into her vortex. Maybe I was lonely, desperate, or dead in the part of my brain that regulated common sense, but I rode every wave.

The more time I spent with her, the more of her true colors began to shine. I knew I had to stop seeing her, but I feared the consequences of doing so. I was afraid of what she would do if I called it off. So, it got to the point where I endured her flip-flopping to keep up appearances and prevent a devastating fallout—not because I enjoyed her companionship. When I couldn't take it anymore and broke up with her, I was transparent about my reasons. Since I wasn't leaving the church, and I had no right to ask her to leave the church, I prayed for a peaceful breakup. I should have known Natalie wouldn't play it cool.

Enough time has passed by now. Natalie should be over it. I'm beginning to wonder if she needs therapy, because her bitterness over our split was undermining my work at the church. Every Sunday, she's in my face scrutinizing something.

One Sunday, she said the topic I chose for the Sunday school lesson was not appropriate for children. The next Sunday, when I was to give my first sermon, was no exception to her misconduct.

After service, folks were lining up to shake my hand and congratulate me for doing an exceptional job. I was feeling good. As I was talking to a parishioner, I could see Natalie approaching in my peripheral vision. She whispered loudly that my fly was down and walked away, laughing hysterically.

A flush immediately crept across my face, and my breathing became rapid. I was beyond embarrassed. I'm sure she sat on the edge of her seat in anticipation, waiting for the end of service so that she could tell me. What a blow to the euphoria I felt, having gotten through my first sermon but only thinking of how humiliating it was to have my fly open the whole time.

She's such a… I won't say it. I probably should talk to the pastor and see if he needs to intervene. One thing's for sure. I'm glad we never had sex. Having sex would have made things way more complicated. Let's see what she'll want to scrutinize and harass me about next Sunday.

*—Seminarian 12*

# S.O.S from a Lonely, Single Seminarian

Dear Diary,

It's that time of year again. Easter week is upon us. Since the start of Lent, I've finally mastered the perfect intonation, pacing, and concise language of my "I have plans" elevator speech for declining Easter Sunday dinner invitations. I've been practicing in the mirror to make sure I'm able to convey sincerity nonverbally. I know the parishioners mean well, but I wish men didnt ask me to be honest. That way, I wouldn't have to decline anybody's invites.

My plans for Sunday are to devour an entire pan of tuna casserole, getting a sugar high from a bag of jellybeans and stretching out on my sofa with a romance novel, or binge watching something on Netflix. Sunday isn't even here yet, and I'm already envisioning my swift and strategic departure from the church grounds to get home.

I wonder what other single students at my school go through

regarding their personal life outside of the church and their studies. I can't be the only one finding it difficult to cope with the external pressures. It would be nice to have at least one person to talk to about this, but I don't know where to start looking to find somebody. I sometimes feel that there's some secret society of seminarians that meet underground.

It's tough being a single seminarian. But I am truly happy. I think there's so much pressure on me to find a partner. I'm afraid to ask other students about their love lives. It's probably not as big of a deal as I'm making it out to be, but I don't feel safe opening up right now. I pray I can get over my anxiety and let God place the right person on my path who can be a sounding board.

I don't mind being single and independent. It suits me well. I'm not in seminary to start a relationship with anybody other than the Almighty and serve as a teacher, counselor, healer, and leader to my congregation. Anything outside of that is secondary. Is it wrong of me to not want to tether myself to a boyfriend or husband? I just want to study, learn and serve.

–Seminarian 13

# Dating App Shuffle: Love with a Swipe Left or Swipe Right

Dear Diary,

Dating apps and online dating sites used to be a trend. People were skeptical about the possibility of finding love with the internet. There were undoubtedly justifiable reasons for being reluctant to create a profile, since it brought out all sorts of predators, con artists, and catfish.

Now dating apps and websites are accepted more, as they have made it more convenient to meet people. I think it's a convenient way to connect with others. It feels like I'm on Amazon shopping for a coffeemaker sometimes. I can specify and filter by what I'm interested in or attracted to with the swipe of a finger with online dating.

I try to keep my profile updated. Even though it is convenient, it also can be risky. Sometimes, you won't know who you will end up meeting. Some nights are better than others. Lately, I've been getting a lot of pings, winks, flirts, and likes.

Honestly, I don't think I'll find the man of my dreams online. But my girlfriend, Ebony, thinks she has found love in Liberia. I'm not fond of long-distance relationships, personally. If you aren't in the same area code or at least within five miles of my zip code, then I'm not interested. That's just me. I want my partner to be accessible and, if need be, on-call for a quickie, kiss, or a hug.

Ebony says she's in love with this guy, but he is having trouble getting a visa to enter America. I'm a bit skeptical. They plan on getting married. It brings to mind the plenty of men in prison with a life sentence who promise women marriage only to keep their commissary abundant. As long as Ebony continues to send this man money nearly every week, what's a real reason for him to move to the US? Ebony believes the money she's sending her overseas boyfriend is going towards a house he's building in Liberia. She told me he has adopted several children in his neighborhood, and her money supports them as well.

I don't know how much she wires to him, but Ebony says it also supports her boyfriend's daily living and education, as he is in a degree program there. To my knowledge, they've never met in person. So, that means all that my generous friend is getting in return for the hard-earned money she sends to a grown man residing in a completely different hemisphere of the globe are his stories of how the money is spent and how he will use it down the road. It doesn't seem fair, if you ask me.

There are plenty of local men who can support Ebony and spend time with her in a tangible reality instead of an entirely virtual one. If she's happy, that's all that matters, right? It's her life. I just don't want to see her getting hurt, especially when it sounds like she's being taken advantage of.

I'm praying that if this man is conning her, the truth reveals itself before she leaves the country next month. I and a few other of her friends at the seminary are planning a going-away party. She's already gotten the green light for a transfer to the school's distance learning program so she can continue with her studies. There's so much at risk, and I want to say something, but I worry that I'll come across as a hater trying to steal her joy. Godspeed, Ebony.

*–Seminarian 14*

# Sinful Sex vs. Blissful Sex

Dear Diary,

I love having sex and lots of it. It's a trait I'm not too fond of about myself. I know I shouldn't leave any room in my body for self-hatred or shame, but no matter how incredible the sex or rapturous the orgasm, the immense feeling of guilt that weighs on me afterward is unbearable. I'm doing some work to start accepting myself for who I am and what I do without harsh self-criticism. Every morning, I lock eyes with my reflection in the mirror. I say, "Kayla, I forgive you for judging me and making me feel like I'm dirty and unclean because I'm a Christian who enjoys having multiple sex partners." I repeat this mantra three times a day to clear my heart chakra and release the baggage of my past I still lug around.

Without self-forgiveness, I would live in torment. But is it forgiveness that I truly need? Is my sexual appetite and behavior such a bad thing? To be honest, I'm confused about the matter. I'm getting conflicting messages from good sources of wisdom and knowledge.

On the one hand, my pastor says that I should suppress my sexual fluidity as a seminarian. I should remain chaste and avoid dating to honor my body, since it is a temple of God. On the other hand, my spiritual life coach says that sex is an expression of personal spirituality and if I wanted a "boy toy" or, depending on the day, a "playgirl," it is natural, and I'm doing nothing wrong. She tells me it is healthy. It can't be both, can it?

I don't want to settle down. No way am I ready to offer my fidelity to only one person. One day I'm sure the right woman or man will come into view, but I just want to have fun right now. Why would God give us sexual fire and desire that feels so good, only for us to ignore it and tame the primal urges? I can't make sense of it.

Suppressing my sexuality is like killing part of myself that must wait indefinitely for resurrection. God, please help me to see this in a way that is honorable and true. I can't entirely ignore the call of my loins, nor can I bear to live in shame for being the person I am. Please, let this cup pass from me. Lord, I am sorry if I disappointed you.

–*Seminarian 15*

# You'd Be the First!

Dear Diary,

I asked Chad to be my "first. He said he would think about it and he would contact me when he decided. I'm turning twenty-seven next month.

—Seminarian 16

# Cheers to Skype! Who Needs In-Person Dates When Virtual Ones Are Better?

Dear Diary,

Romantic relationships are exhausting, but that doesn't mean I don't want to be in one. I've changed in many ways since my last relationship. Because of past experiences, I want to offer myself as a better person to my next partner.

Recently, I created a profile on a dating app and signed up for Skype. I hope that having these accounts will help me find someone special. I'm putting a lot of faith in this virtual approach to dating. Meeting in person takes up too much of my time.

Meeting people online is safer for me, and I have more control over my experience. For example, suppose I start to feel uncomfortable, bored, or whatever adverse feeling that could come up during the online date. In that case, I can do something like turn off the wi-fi or mute the guy, especially if he starts talking too much about himself. I just have to try not to yawn. I've gotten quicker at turning off the camera briefly if I feel a yawn building.

Anyway, with virtual dates, I have more time to do my seminary studies. In general, dates are time-consuming, but they also require a lot of effort on my part. I've rarely had a good enough in-person date with a man that made me feel the time and exertion was worth it. Some guys I meet on the app are okay with a virtual date, but most men would prefer to meet in person. Every date I go on takes away valuable study time. If the date ends up being an epic disaster, then I will feel bad for prioritizing my love life above that of my schoolwork, which should mean more than anything else at this time.

The great thing about the dating app is that I'm no longer apprehensive about accepting an invitation to go on a date. Also, it takes some pressure off me on virtual dates because I don't have to worry about the reaction to seeing me in a wheelchair. Online dates give me and the other person I'm talking to more time to cultivate a healthy relationship founded on getting to know each other first before revealing that I have a physical disability that confines me to a wheelchair.

Knowing my personality and liking me as Dee softens the initial shock many guys have when they see my wheels. I realize the full package is a lot. I used to get offended when I would go out with a man who couldn't accept all of me. Now, I just brush off shallow men, but I can understand that to accept me—a wheelchair-bound seminary student preparing to be a messenger of God—might be too much to take in all at once.

I enjoy my classes at the seminary, and it's the most important thing going on with me right now, but I long for love. I'm convinced that if I could just find the right guy, I could balance school and romance.

I often wonder if being single when you don't want to be is karmic punishment for bad choices and relationships in the past. After all, relational disconnection is not what God had in mind when he created Adam and Eve. So, what am I to do, when what I want to be is a Mrs.? I'm still praying and waiting on the Lord. I'm hoping that he will answer my prayer through online dating.

*–Seminarian 17*

# Not Another Sext Message? Dude, Put Some Clothes On, Please

Dear Diary,

I'm trying my best to be the bigger person right now, but John's racy texts trigger me. I admit that getting a sexy message or nude pic from your partner helps spice up the relationship by building up desire. When John used to sex text me at first while I was in class at the seminary, the image would give me something to look forward to after class for that day. But now it's become excessive.

We're still getting to know each other, but if he doesn't stop sending me these nudes all day, I'm pretty sure we wouldn't be able to have a long-term relationship ever. He wants to "do it to me." I get it. Sending naked pics was hot the first time. I sent him one back. The second time he sent one, it was kind of cute. But the third, thirteenth and thirtieth picture of his penis is borderline disgusting. I've had it! Plus, he sends these sexy texts when he knows I'm in class.

Yesterday, I was sitting with three other students working on a group project in our hermeneutics class. Out of nowhere, he tried to video call me and was naked. I should have had my phone off while I was in class, but because my phone was out, I know the others saw him on the screen. It was so embarrassing. I'm glad I have mature classmates. They diverted their attention and didn't snicker or gasp. There was just an awkward silence. I played it off and continued working. Now, I put my phone on "Do not disturb" when I'm in class. John must understand I'm in school to learn, and I shouldn't open myself to distractions. Intimacy in person is a much better option.

*–Seminarian 18*

# God's Most Embarrassing Messenger and the Boyfriend Who Has the Receipts

*Dear Diary,*

*I'm trying my best to cool down. Even though my* flared nostrils, tense muscles, palpitating heart, and sound of my breathing overshadowing my thoughts all say I'm pissed, I'm trying to be calm. I just had another argument with Stephan. My antidepressants aren't necessarily engineered for this type of emotion and physiology. So, I know I'm pushing things to their limits. Still, I've got to get in control of this anger, or else I'll end up only validating my boyfriend's claims that I'm an embarrassment to the Most High, to myself, and to my career goals after graduating from seminary.

How can he say that? Those words are probably some of the most insensitive and hurtful words your lover or anybody close to you can speak. Just because I get angry easily over stupid, sometimes petty things doesn't give him the right to judge me. Who does he think he is? Just because I may have overreacted to some grade school, he-said-she-said drama he brought up doesn't mean that I'm not worthy of being a worker for God.

So, what if I just sent him thirty text messages? I had to defend myself. I needed to make sure he heard me. I want to scream! Doesn't he know how much I'm hurting right now? Should I send him another message? No, wait. I shouldn't do that. It would only be more evidence for his prosecution. Even though I don't understand why he's criminalizing my feelings.

Now that I'm sitting here and putting it in black and white, my breathing has returned to normal, and I've stopped grinding my teeth, I can see that there was a better way to handle things. Everything escalated quickly because I let my anger issues get the best of me. I have to learn how to be slow to anger.

Seminarians aren't saints, but we are held to a higher standard than most people. Being in a romantic relationship is difficult as it is without having one partner who probably needs an anger management class. It doesn't help if the other partner has no degree of emotional intelligence, empathy, or compassion to know that you don't tell someone preparing for a lifetime of servitude to God Almighty that they are unworthy.

Thirty irate, hypersensitive, emotional texts or not, you just don't say things like that. I need more self-control. I'm working on it, but I can't help but wonder if there was some truth in his insults. Maybe I am an embarrassment to God. Perhaps I don't deserve to be in the seminary. I feel so bad. Lord, help me regulate my emotions.

*–Seminarian 19*

# To the Moon, Ella!
# To the Moon!

Dear Diary,

If there is one thing that a person could do to me that instantly triggers my blood's boiling with irrational anger, it is ghosting. I don't particularly appreciate texts going unanswered or my calls being sent to voicemail. It's childish. I haven't heard from my girlfriend in three days. I'm done! Trying to juggle my course work and a romantic relationship is much harder than I thought. I'm on edge all the time and can't find any peace of mind. Dealing with Ella's crap isn't helping. I've been unhappy for some time now. I was waiting for the perfect opportunity to end things, I guess. This stunt is it.

What reason could she have for ghosting me? If anybody should be the one ghosted, it's Ella! She criticizes everything, from how I dress to my choice of occupation. If she has a problem with me being a man of the cloth, why is she going out with me?

During these three days without any communication between us, I've had a chance to assess our relationship. More specifically, I've been trying to justify ending it with her. My friends all tried to tell me that she and I weren't compatible. I didn't listen because, for lack of a better term, I was sprung.

I should have looked harder at what I was getting involved with by messing around with her. If I had been thinking with my intelligence and not my hormones, I would've known I was damned from the start getting involved with an aggressive woman like Ella—a girl who doesn't know when to shut up or how to speak using an inside voice. All her annoying ways only are amplified when she is boozing and we're hanging out with her friends. Not even my mother loud-talks to me. But Ella likes to do it all the time, and for some reason, I let her. She has a dominant personality that has benefits in only certain circumstances but not all the time. It's like she's trying to emasculate me. I deserve better than that. Even when we're around her folks, she talks over me. Maybe her parents had that kind of dynamic in their home when she was growing up. I don't know, but I know I'm not used to it. It certainly wasn't like that with my folks.

I have to use a lot of restraint to tolerate the things Ella does. I must be a fool to sacrifice my happiness to maintain a relationship with a woman who lies about where she spends her time and who she's with. I've got studies to think about and a future as a minister to prepare for.

I don't need to depreciate the quality of my life for some belligerent woman who doesn't have the courtesy or respect to answer the phone when I call. That's it! I've made up my mind. I'm calling all this off whenever she returns my calls. I just have to make sure I'm calm when she does, or else I might jump through the phone and punch her in the throat, sending her to the moon like Ralph Kramden from *The Honeymooners*. Forgive me, Lord. I didn't mean that. I'm just fed up.

—*Seminarian* 20

# She Wasn't Saving Herself for Marriage, She was Saving Herself for Another Woman

Dear Diary,

I can be as patient as the next seminarian when it comes to celibacy. My girlfriend told me she didn't want to have sex until she was married. I respected that and didn't pressure her. There's more to a relationship than having sex. Without physical intimacy complicating things, Jackie and I built a firm foundation for our relationship that brought us closer and gave us a chance to appreciate each other. At least, that's what I thought. I finally understand what it means to have the wool pulled over one's eyes.

Over five months of dinners together, movie nights, walks in the park, handholding on the seminary campus, and 1,001 conversations about our plans for the future, it never crossed my mind to ask my girl if she was a lesbian. So, you can imagine the jaw-dropping astonishment I had when she confessed that she could never be happy with me because she likes women. She went on to say that we had to break up because she had found a girl on campus who she wanted to be with.

Her confession was disillusioning, because I had often wondered how a woman as fine as she was, with the sweetest disposition that could instantly give you diabetes and an intelligence that was borderline genius, had been single as long as she claimed. It seems she only dated me as a covert attempt to delude the congregation where she interned. It turns out that the other woman is in my apologetics class, who I almost asked out before getting with Jackie. The irony of it all.

Jackie's lying hurt me because she essentially used me—not for my body, but my gender. There were other women I could have dated during those five months. There was a lot of sex that I could've been having as well. Not to mention, I could have spent more time focusing on my studies and strengthening my relationship with the Father.

I wish her well, but I'll be too embarrassed to tell another soul the real reason for our breakup. To think, I'd finally found someone I felt safe enough with to let my guard down and be vulnerable within a new relationship, despite the sickening anxiety I felt while doing it. Guess I should have taken heed of that anxiety.

*–Seminarian 21*

# Since We Just Broke Up Today, Do I Still Have to Preach for Your Congregation Tomorrow? ... Awkward

Dear Diary,

Well, it's official, Nick and I are done. I have to admit, his attempts to cover his tracks were quite brilliant. He created dummy social media accounts and got friends and family to lie and everything. All the energy and time, even money he spent to ensure a successful deception, took cheating to a whole new level. I was somewhat impressed by his conniving behind. But just as intelligent as he was, to the same degree, he was a fool. Did he think this child of God would not find out? It's downright laughable when I think about it. Glory be to the Father, who brought everything to light. Once all the pieces fell into place, and I discovered the truth, I called him up and broke up with him. Don't get me wrong. I'm going to miss him and the love we made, but I can't put up with a man who is a professional liar and cheat. I deserve better.

When I dialed him a few hours ago to break up with him, my emotions were so high that I temporarily forgot I was supposed to preach at his church tomorrow. I guess I could have ignored him today or come up with some reason for not being around to get through the sermon on Sunday, and then have broken up with him after service.

I don't want to start singing the "should've-could've-would've" blues. I need some damage control ASAP. I don't want to see him tomorrow or his Acura with personalized plates in the church's parking lot, let alone stand in front of his congregation and preach a sermon of deliverance. Can we say, "awkward?" This happens to be the church where we met. I love his church family, but I don't want to see any of them either. To top it off, the couple that introduced us to one another, Bobby and Sarah, I'm sure will be there also.

I'm feeling a little anxiety creeping in. My throat feels a little scratchy all of a sudden. I don't think being a guest minister at his congregation tomorrow is a good idea. I guess I'm going to call out sick. The breakup is too fresh for me to have to see his cheating face again. I'm not ready.

*—Seminarian 22*

# My Facebook Says "Divorce," and My Ring Finger Is Bare: You Do the Math

## Dear Diary,

Should I make a formal announcement that Carlos and I are getting a divorce? He moved out of our home three months ago, and it's been that long since he's made an appearance at the church. No one has asked me any direct questions about my marriage, but I see how the parishioners keep checking my hand to see if I am still wearing my wedding ring.

Even though I think my personal life is none of anybody's business, I don't like lying to my congregation. After all, I am a public figure. Many church members are friends on my Facebook, and I want to change my relationship status to single. I'd rather let the congregation draw their own conclusions. Do I really need to announce my business in front of my entire church? I feel like I'm a contradiction to all the marriage counseling I've given. Can't I let everyone put two and two together? Seminary taught me a lot about theology, but I didn't learn how to navigate divorce and lead a congregation at the same time.

I never thought my marriage would come to an end. I never believed in divorce. I've always believed in the sanctity of marriage vows. Despite the unified front of marital bliss at church, we just couldn't make it work.

Honestly, now that the marriage is over, I'm looking forward to being single again. I will be able to travel more often with my friends. I'll have the freedom to meet new people and start new platonic and romantic relationships. However, what I'm most looking forward to, with my marriage in ashes, is the opportunity to get back in touch with myself and be myself without having to consider if I am too much or not enough for anyone else.

—Seminarian 23

# Be Careful What You Pray for, Because You Will Get It

## Dear Diary,

I'm dating two women right now. Both of the ladies attend the same seminary as I do. I'm in a few classes with them, but they aren't in any with each other. I made sure of that. Both women are attractive, smart, and have led "interesting" lives that make them more unique than any other women I've dated. I like that they represent specific values and beliefs similar to mine and share a reverence for God. But it's time for me to drop one and pursue a long-term relationship with the other. I just don't know which one. The more time I spend with each woman, the more drawn I am to them. I've never felt so indecisive in my life.

Before getting involved with these women, I prayed to God, asking for someone to enter my life who was "interesting." So, the Lord saw fit first to send me Laura, a girl who learned how to swallow knives so she could join the circus before enrolling in the seminary. In the same week, the Lord Most High placed Tina on my path, who told me she is a multilevel marketer who hosts sex toy parties that currently pay for her seminary education.

These "interesting" but borderline weird women are breathtakingly beautiful and keep surprising me on every date with their fascinating stories. I don't know if I should choose one of them, neither, or return to my knees for prayer. I've gotten what I asked for and can genuinely say they both are heaven-sent, but who should I give the rose to, like in that ridiculous reality show, *The Bachelor?* Next time, I'll need to be more specific about what I want in my prayers.

—*Seminarian* 24

# Mom, There's a Reason My "Roommate" and I Share a Bed

*Dear Diary,*

*My partner and I have been together for three* years. We have decided to take our relationship to the next level and live together. In a culture that has homogenized shacking up and made it acceptable, this shouldn't be a big deal, right? Wrong. It's not all that simple when you're a lesbian couple living in a one-bedroom apartment on the campus of an orthodox seminary that upholds conservative family values, and your mother plans to visit and meet your girlfriend, who she thinks is just a roommate.

I love Elizabeth, but her moving in with me—something that millions of unwed and gay people do all the time—has the potential to wreck my peaceful life or rather the facade of one. I decided to attend this school because my mom is alumni, and the rent for an apartment is cheap. I have not come out of the closet to my mom yet, and she thinks my partner is my roommate. I haven't told her that I have a one-bedroom apartment. My mom is coming to visit next week. I don't know how this is going to turn out.

*—Seminarian 25*

# The Loneliness Hurts, But I'd Rather Be Alone

Dear Diary,

Holidays have been rough for me since the car crash that killed Tristan five years ago. Sometimes I wish it had been my life that was taken. I'm working on self-forgiveness. I know that the Lord spared my life to fulfill my calling to His service as a minister. I miss her so much. I took to drinking to cope with the grief and loss, and holidays used to be an excuse for getting wasted. She was the love of my life. Correction: She will always be the love of my life. Only the Savior's love can fill the emptiness I feel. I have nightmares still, but each day I grow stronger. I'm in recovery now and talk therapy to work on my survivor's guilt. I'm glad to say I have more constructive ways of coping than hitting the bottle.

Because so much has been taken from me, I choose to give instead during this time of year. This Thanksgiving, I decided not to go home and will stay on campus. The seminary seems so empty, but I'm fixing a nice meal that I'll share with a few homeless families. I want to spend Thanksgiving at home alone. I have to learn how to be content and comfortable with solitude.

A classmate invited me to come to her apartment for "Friendsgiving." She's a sweet girl. I've thought about asking her out, but I have too many wounds that haven't healed. I'm a little fickle when it comes to dating. Part of me wants to get back out there and date again, but I think it's more important to focus on loving myself. I don't think dating is the right thing for me right now.

*—Seminarian 26*

# Boundaries, Please: Us Having Coffee Together Isn't a Reason to Pry into My Personal Life

Dear Diary,

So, it is finally starting to happen. Parishioners are feeling the need to confront me about my private life. It was bound to happen eventually, I guess. It's partly my fault, because I often bring my dates to church. The way I see it, if I'm going to be with a man, he has to be supportive of me at the church and demonstrate a reverence to God. What better way to have more than just "pillow talk" than to invite someone I'm dating to the church so we could have profound discussions about the word of God as well?

Anyway, from the outside peeking in, I can imagine what it may look like. But honestly, I don't see why it's anybody's business. One parishioner commented on the different "special guests" I've brought to the church. So, what? Then another member had something to say about me being unmarried. Only God can judge, but others try. One member implied that I have a reputation around town for being with lots of men. I don't know who's talking, but now I know I'm being talked about—and not about my sermons. Then, there's yet another parishioner who whispered to me, "Don't cha get lonely living in that big ol' house by yourself?" I told him it didn't bother me and that a husband wasn't on my mind. Technically, I realize, it's lying, but I was just trying to establish boundaries.

I'm trying my best to keep my romantic affairs and personal life to myself and whichever man I'm dating. I spend hours upon hours flirtatiously chatting with guys on this dating app called Hinge. If I thought it was anybody's business, I would stand at the pulpit next Sunday and proclaim, "I'm fifty, single, and interning at this church as part of my education at the seminary. Just like each member of the congregation, my steps are ordered by God, and no one needs to comment, imply, or intend to make gradual inroads into my personal life."

I think about marriage all the time. That's why some nights I can't sleep. I sometimes stay on Facebook until three a.m., responding to posts just to feel connected to someone. I want a husband more than the well-meaning members want me to find one, but I don't think it is appropriate for me to discuss that with them. Let them speculate all they want. I have my life to live, and they have theirs. So, I hope they will spend more time focusing on themselves instead of my special guests on any given Sunday. God bless them.

*—Seminarian 27*

# Hopeless Hater and Begrudged Bachelorette

Dear Diary,

This summer, I officiated two weddings for my friends. They were two beautiful celebrations of love.

I'm ceaselessly working my body to the bone, a sacrificial lamb devoted to the service of helping others in need all around me. I give and give. When's the day of my reckoning, when I too will receive the same degree that I give? I deserve good things as well. I must suffer silently. I'm drowning in the anguish of a lonely, loveless life. Because I'm the minister in my circle of friends, I'm not supposed to feel this way, but I'm also a woman—one who needs amorous affection, attention, and tenderness. Whose arms can I run into?

—Seminarian 28

# I'm the Great Pretender, But for How Long?

Dear Diary,

My depression has reached new levels this semester, and it's causing an immense, overwhelming feeling that I can't take. It's all these darn "call" meetings that I'm attending that are escalating my depressive symptoms. It's so exhausting and wreaks havoc on my self-esteem. I feel it lowering with each interview. I'm so solicitous about receiving approval by the committee that I'm in extraordinary duress when I have to face several strangers attempting to convince them of my worthiness. How on earth can I convince a person or group of persons who don't know me from Adam of all my goodness and integrity?

Most times, I believe there is nothing about myself that is worthwhile. So, each rejection only validates my feelings of insignificance. I feel like a statue made entirely of cellophane when

I'm in front of these panels of people who hold power to change my life either positively or negatively, and that they see right through me. I have to put up a decent show that gives the impression that I'm the "perfect" pastoral candidate for the church. As I respond to their questions, I struggle with every bit of my heart internally, as this voice keeps objecting to my claims of excellence with snide remarks like, "Yeah, right, Felicia," and "Who do you think you're fooling? You're a nobody."

I'm starting to believe I'm nowhere near to being good enough for a congregation. I find myself dwelling in a constant state of inner turmoil and madness. My desire to be the "perfect" pastor has created the "perfect" hell within my mind, body, and spirit. If it's not in front of the selection committee for those "call" interrogations, I'm having to deal with my family and friends hounding me about getting married.

Why would I want to invite a man into my life that's under constant attack by depression and anxiety? I don't need the pressure of finding a mate. I just want to be good enough for myself without having to go on dates and dating apps trying to convince strange men that I'm all the woman they need. It is such a nefarious life I live. I don't know how much more I can take. What kind of wife or pastor will I be when my true dark, depressive colors shine through after I've grown weary of pretending to be a perfect choice?

*—Seminarian 27*

# Doomed to Never Forget Him on V-Day

*Dear Diary,*

*It sucks when something horrible happens on* holidays. Getting dumped on an average day feels terrible enough, but a person most likely won't celebrate its anniversary every year. However, having your heart broken on a day like Valentine's Day, you'll be reminded of the breakup every single year. You'll have to watch as the rest of the country celebrates their love, as if gloating with boisterous store displays, radio station dedications, candies, cards, and balloons everywhere you turn—even at your school. That's my story.

The anniversary of the split last year with Chad will live on in my memory with annual reminders of a love loss anniversary, while millions of couples celebrate how their love lives on. Stupid holiday! I want to tear down all the Valentine's Day decorations at the seminary. Ugh! Can't I just hibernate until February 15th? Last February 14th was the most supernaturally lousy day of my life. Unless I find love again, every Valentine's Day will stain my memory in perpetuity.

–Seminarian 30

# The War on Terror Is Over, But I'm Still in Terror Fighting Demons Every Day

Dear Diary,

I'm having trouble transitioning from the military back into civilian life. I was diagnosed with PTSD just before coming to the seminary. I disclosed my condition to the school during my interview. I'm so grateful they didn't hold it against me, which is more than I can say for my family and my church's pastor. Although my "G.I. Jane" days are over, I still want to serve the country by becoming a military chaplain. I want to talk openly to my family about my struggle with PTSD, but I can't. I come from a patriotic, Christian family that believes living with a mental illness is a sign of spiritual weakness. From the lens they use to view the world, their solution is to repent for any sins I committed while serving my country. I know they would tell me to look to God for my healing. I have, but I still have PTSD.

My pastor said that my mental illness is a result of a demonic attack on me. I was baptized in the church when I returned from my second tour in Afghanistan. If I denounced Satan already, why do I still feel like an awful person? I've yet to get the memories out of my head. Sometimes, I think the demon is me.

Recently, I had a situation with this guy I was dating. He triggered my PTSD symptoms, and I got stuck in my emotions as a result. I realize now I might have been harassing him with all the calls and texts, but I couldn't get my impulsiveness in check to save my life. I've had a lot of problems with men as I suffer from this condition. Before coming to the seminary, on more than one occasion the men I went out with would comment that I have a complex personality. I can't argue with that. They also called me a crazy bitch. They haven't seen crazy. Many people don't understand the long-lasting effects of unprocessed trauma, but I'm grateful to the seminary for all the support they've given to me. They have shown a lot of support to the veteran community in general.

I still have flashbacks from serving in Afghanistan. I feel like I'm always on edge. Loud noises make me jumpy. That's another thing about the school I like, the quietness on campus. I'm also grateful to have a few "battle buddies" I stay in contact with from the army. Unfortunately, I haven't met anyone on campus with whom I can comfortably share my experience.

—Seminarian 31

# I Love Being in My Company, Because I Love and Respect Myself

Dear Diary,

Saturday, I performed my first wedding. It was a beautiful event. Sincere happiness filled my heart to witness two beautiful creatures of God who had found love and chose to stand before their closest family and friends to declare their devotion and vow their fidelity to each other. Mind you, at this time last year being single at a wedding would have caused me great sadness and pain. I used to think it was a curse to live from day to day with only the companionship of me, myself, and I.

Don't get me wrong—sometimes, the most challenging part of being single is pushing through the bad times alone. The single life gets old really fast then. The same could be said about being alone during the good times as well. Just as I would love a hand to hold when in turmoil, life has so many good things to offer that I would love to have someone to share them with.

I've grown so much over the years. I have no regrets, fears, shame, or self-pity for being a minister, remaining single by choice. If a time comes when being single no longer pleases me, I trust in the love I would have cultivated within myself during my time alone to be shared with someone who deserves it.

*-Seminarian 32*

# New Year's Fling at the Center of the World

*Dear Diary,*

*A singles group at the seminary is coordinating a* singles trip. I'm so excited. I purchased a ticket the minute they announced it! Who knows who might be waiting for me. I might meet someone special. Lately, I've been practicing how to disclose that I'm a seminarian to men I'm on a date with. I'm graduating soon. So, I'll be clergy officially and can't see how I could keep it a secret. At least for now, I can just say I'm a student without mentioning a connection to religion if I don't want to.

I have a feeling my dating life will change dramatically once I've graduated and become a bona fine lady of the cloth. Would someone even think about dating a clergy? I mean, this is not an episode of *Sex in the City*, and I'm a far cry from the show's main character, Carrie. Sex is such a beautiful experience. It's a shame it's such a taboo word.

I grew up in a Pentecostal church, and the only time I heard about sex was in the gossiping whispers throughout the church during a sex scandal that rocked the pews.

I now have my own beliefs about sex. The singles trip is right after Christmas, during the week approaching New Year's. I hope I find a nice guy there at the center of the world. I can see it now. What a lovely way to start the year. I can hardly wait!

*–Seminarian 33*

# Ordinarily, I Wouldn't Judge, but Today, I'm Judging

*Dear Diary,*

*Nick told me he used to sell marijuana on the side* to "earn a little extra cash." I felt like I had landed in a scene of that show *Breaking Bad*. I couldn't believe it when he told me. Why did this grown, intelligent, good-looking, spiritual man need to sell drugs? I didn't say the first thing that came to mind, which was, "What the hell is wrong with getting a part-time job?" I stayed quiet at first, but it was an immediate turnoff.

I realize that selling drugs can be quite lucrative, but that didn't make it any less illegal. I watched drugs ruin my community and destroy the lives of some of my relatives. Who's to say that when the country's next recession hits, he won't return to his dealer ways? I knew at that moment that I could no longer date him. He purposely put narcotics in the hands of people who couldn't find healthier ways to live their lives—possibly, indirectly making him responsible for the decline of their lives. He might've even sold to children. Surely young people can't see past a high into their future to know better.

I have no place to judge him for things he did before meeting me, but I can't forgive them in the present. I understand, he was young and dumb, but I couldn't see past his past. He might've changed since then, but confessing about his dangerous profession was too much for this minister to bear. I'm sorry.

Nick can be upset with me if he wants to, but as a woman first and a preacher second, selling drugs is a moral offense I can't forgive. Maybe I have some growing to do, and perhaps I'm bailing out on a chance to be with an otherwise good, upstanding guy. I just can't deal. He asked me if God had forgiven him for what he did. I told him I had a call on the other line. I couldn't answer that question at that moment.

*–Seminarian 34*

# There's No Way Your Mother Can Live with Us

*Dear Diary,*

*Rick ended our engagement. I had a creepy feeling* that he was going to dump me after our last fight. We fought over his mom coming to live with us next year after we get married. His mom has dementia. I believe she should go live in an assisted living facility. We already had a conversation about children. I told him I wasn't ready. So, taking care of an aging adult, which would nearly require me to take on the same responsibilities as child-rearing, was undoubtedly out of the question.

I realize how callous and cold-hearted my stance on the issue sounds. Still, he doesn't understand that a parent with dementia can be a full-time job, especially when the parent has a history of wandering, falling, and injuring herself. Furiously, he said I'm not the "Christian woman" he thought I was, but I stood behind my words. He expected me to understand what he felt was his obligation to his mother. I reminded Rick how his mom burned her arm last week because she was trying to cook. I cannot deal with the stress of caring for his mom, planning a wedding, and attending all my seminary classes.

His sister is currently caring for their mom, but she is burned out. Who wouldn't be? Rick's sister says it's a big ordeal just for her to go to the grocery store or grab lunch with a friend without deserting her caregiver duties. I don't want to lose him, but truthfully, I'm too focused on my career right now. I hope he finds the "Christian woman" he is looking for.

—Seminarian 35

# We're Good—Oral Sex Is the Next Best Thing

Dear Diary,

I woke up last night on the couch next to Dan. Despite our strong attraction to each other, we didn't have sex per se. We fooled around with kisses and caresses, and he pleasured me orally. It was nice. I know he wanted more. So, did I, but I've already told him I'm not having sex until I'm married.

Once I started seminary, I vowed to consecrate myself to my studies and abstain from frivolous fornication until my wedding night. Dan had been respectful of my celibacy, and last night was the farthest we'd taken our passions without giving in to the deepest desires to get it on.

Before seminary, I had lots of sex, but abstinence was something I had to do for myself to feel clean before God as I prepared to be a leader of his people. I still have desires, and Dan enjoys sex as much as I do. My only fear is that he'll grow frustrated without having complete fulfillment in our relationship from physical intimacy, and he'll suffer to the point of looking elsewhere to satisfy his appetite. We decided that oral sex would provide us both pleasure without penetration. Oral sex isn't sex, right? So, I don't think it's anything I need to be ashamed of. I hope I'm still showing faithfulness to the promise I made to myself.

It disturbs me that I don't know for sure if having oral sex is considered just as sinful as premarital sex. I'm in freaking seminary, for crying out loud. If anyone should know, surely a seminarian should. I am not alone, either. Many seminarians wonder the same thing as well. Two of my classmates, Megan and Kristine, told me they only allow intimate touching and oral sex with their boyfriends. They said that they are not doing anything wrong because it is only arousal and no penetration. Ugh! Why does it have to be so darn confusing?

I remember my health education teacher in high school telling us that "oral sex is not really sex" and is an alternative to sexual intercourse. I have also heard friends refer to oral sex as safer, even though it is still possible to catch an STD. Of course, the ones asking these questions are Christians wondering what is permissible within (yes, some married people still have a problem with it) and outside of the marriage bed. Non-Christians don't ask these questions. They usually don't have the same moral standards nor the Holy Spirit whispering in their ear as they are "getting it on" with someone.

–Seminarian 36

# Holy or UnHoly Transition

*Dear Diary,*

*I am happily single for the first time in my life. I* am finally free to be me. I grew up believing I was a girl. My gender assigned at birth was a boy. I don't consider myself to be male or female. My gender expression is fluid. I am in the midst of a transition, and learning how to present myself to the world as a Queer person right now is my new normal. I am transitioning while attending seminary. It's very complicated, and I desperately need to get clear. I feel like my world is unraveling. I lived as a married man for eighteen years. As a couple, we considered ourselves as allies of the LGBTQIA community. The pandemic was tough on my marriage. It forced us to spend more time together. We have spent the last year on an emotional roller coaster. The lack of social events, gyms, or extended work hours outside of the home forced us to stay at home and face the truth about who we had become and who we have always been secretly. I could no longer hide that I was not attracted to her. I loved her immensely. She is my best friend. My gender dysphoria was at an all-time high when I asked for a divorce. She immediately assumed I was leaving her for another woman. My wife looked defeated when she told me that she always knew that I was gay or something and feared this day would come. She only stayed in our marriage because of our three kids and her religious beliefs. We had a sexless marriage for many years, because I never felt comfortable in my own skin. I simply couldn't get a hard-on in her presence. I would blame it on my diabetes, close my eyes, and think of my favorite actor while rubbing myself against her. I tried oral sex with her, but the taste and smell of a vagina doesn't move me. I still can't believe that we conceived three children together. Our children are very young. I hope they will still embrace me after the transition. Our family has navigated many life changes. We explained to our kids that we are ending our relationship, but we are not ending our family. I felt ashamed that I didn't fit into the conventional, masculine role of being a husband and father or give them the fairytale ending we had hoped for when we married.

I have always been Queer, but I covered it up with my fundamentalist, philosophical, and theological views about God, Adam, and Jesus. I also covered it up with being a workaholic.

I've known that I was Queer since high school, and I married my ex-wife to appear more "manly" to my friends and family. My father-in-law used to joke about me being the best "wife" his daughter could ever have because I enjoyed cooking, interior design, and knitting, and I was very nurturing to our son. He said that my farmer overalls and cowboy boots didn't match well with the plaid apron I loved to wear while baking cookies. I am now single: happily single and free to explore what it means for me to be Queer. I no longer identify as a man. I am taking hormones to soften my features and vocal lessons to decrease my baritone voice. I woke up last night on the couch still wearing the eyeshadow from my makeup class, wondering what my seminary friends were going to think when I begin to identify as Queer.

I wonder if I should identify as nonbinary. I'm still trying to figure it out before I come out to others. My Queerness was not a secret to my mom. I broke the news to her first a couple of months ago, and she told me that it was time for me to stop hiding my authentic self and she always knew because I couldn't do "manly" things very well. I cried like a baby as I confessed that the idea of masculinity doesn't make sense to me. I thought she was going to condemn me to hell for being a shitty son and for not being able to live up to the masculine ideal that I was forced to embrace as a kid. I felt so accomplished after talking to my mom. I never knew my dad. He left my mom before I was born. I never had a consistent male role model in my life, other than Jesus. My church made Jesus seem super masculine at times, but loving and nurturing, too.

We never discussed Jesus's sexuality during Bible study, and the one time I asked if he had a girlfriend; I was told to take a "time out" and go sit in the corner as my punishment. I stopped asking questions after that incident, but I often wondered if Adam was both male and female, since God took a rib from Adam and made Eve. If humans are made in the image and likeness of God, does this mean that God has both masculine and feminine qualities? I don't know the answers to these questions. I can only speculate. I pray my theological studies at seminary and my transition will help me find truth. I am a Christian. I am Queer. I am transitioning to a feminine gender expression. I love Jesus. I am going into ministry without fear of bigotry. God has opened the door for me to attend seminary on a scholarship.

I have faith that it is in God's will for my life to be here studying God's word. I don't expect everyone to understand or embrace my transition. I know God loves me. My presence is not a disruption or distraction in the seminary. I gave my life to Jesus. The Church is my world, but the code of conduct in my church is to disavow homosexuality. I can't find Biblical scripture that says I am supposed to disavow my Queerness. How do I disavow myself while believing that I am a creation of God? This is how God created me. I wasn't sexually abused by a priest, the creepy guy who lived two doors down from us, a family member, or my babysitter. I wasn't turned out by some closeted, gay soldier while I was serving in the Army. This is how I naturally feel on the inside.

I am a part of the "good ole boy" network at my church. The topic of homosexuality is always readily available when someone mentions sin. I know what the Bible says about homosexuality. I've read it several times. Intellectually, I have spent years trying to wrap my head around "a man lying with another man" as being an abomination and serving a God that doesn't make mistakes. Does God think of me, his creation, as an abomination? There is a deep, dark sadness within me that I can't shake, because I don't know. I put up a wall around my authentic self when bonding with men at church. My church denomination has been one of the most outspoken opponents of the LGBTQIA community. They oppose people like me being in ministry, and the best way for me to keep my job at the church is to keep quiet about my divorce and transition until I find an LGBTQIA-friendly congregation. I choose to follow Jesus daily. I love God with all of my heart, mind, and soul. I wake up every morning excited to be God's servant in the world. I am doing the best I know how to serve God as I have been created. In my mind and heart, I am a perfect creation of God, because my God doesn't make mistakes. I am proud to be a Christian. I love Jesus, and I am Queer. I don't know why I was born this way. God knows. I pray that God will change the hearts and minds of His people.

–Seminarian 37

# ~ Conclusion ~

*There you have it. First, for those of you who think* that being single is difficult, pause for a moment and consider the plight of a single seminarian. Seminarians and ordained clergy want to find love and marry rather than struggle with dating. Still, they also experience the same difficulties as the people they serve in their churches. First, as you consider these scenarios, accept that seminarians and ordained clergy are people, just like you. Becoming a seminarian does not take away their lustful desires once they became ordained. Many people struggle with this reality, because they are taught that being "saved" meant that God would take away all their romantic emotions—and leave them pure and holy to get on with saving the world. Ignorance and denial are major factors here. I was taught by the church to suppress my desire to discuss my sexuality and spirituality openly. I grew up in the church believing in the separation of church and state, and the separation of my spirituality and my sexuality.

Hath not a seminarian eyes to see and ears to hear? Hath not a seminarian hands, lips, a vagina, penis, and passions, just as members of the congregation they are called to serve? Yes, we go out on Friday night dates, and we enjoy it. But we enjoy it more if we are somewhere where everyone else does not usually see us. Yes, we get excited about our first dates, meeting a hot guy or a sexy woman in the supermarket and being asked out for dinner.

However, we avoid revealing what we *really* do for a living initially to avoid the judgement of others. I have spent countless hours trying to figure out how to avoid questions about my job and revealing that I am a seminarian on the first date. I want to go out and have a good time with someone without having to hear about how you experienced childhood trauma, the death of your dog, or how you want to be forgiven for stealing your sister's boyfriend in the third grade while in the middle of a date. Such conversations can be a bit of a turn-off for me. I know that I will eventually have to reveal that I am a seminarian, but I hope that someone will give me an opportunity to just be me. I love my work. I understand that my work and me are one. I understand that I have a huge responsibility to care for the souls of people. Trust me, I feel the pressure daily, and I lean on my colleagues for a safe space and support. Ministry is a lifestyle, and how it looks varies from person to person.

I want to be in ministry and live as my authentic self. You know, just as God created me. I've done some desperate things for love as a seminarian. Does this mean that I am unlovable to God? Does this mean that God will abandon me? Does this mean that I am unfit to be a minister and serve God's people? Does this make me a hypocrite? Will God punish me for giving in to flesh? Have I angered God by having such thoughts and desires? Will God withhold His love and promises from me because of my sexual promiscuity while I was in seminary?

These are the questions that keep me up late at night. Is the loss of my job, financial trouble, the death of my dad, and or my recent diagnosis of multiple sclerosis a result of my disobedience to God? Am I now on God's hit list? These are the questions I ask God daily.

I pray and repent daily, but I ask myself, *Is it enough?* Am I enough for ministry? Or am I too much? Am I worthy of the clergy collar? Do the things I find most pleasurable in my life please God?

I must admit that sometimes it is painful to be present and sit with my questions, but I must do it because I am expected to be "expert" on the subject matter for members of my future congregation. For some of my colleagues, the pressure of being a seminarian and becoming an ordained minister was too much. I had several classmates quit and return to their "normal" jobs, such as teaching, working in corporate America, or even retail. Sadly, we had three students commit suicide because of the challenges they were facing in their personal lives.

These are the stories that people don't hear about us, and so often when they do, they judge us. I am a servant of God. I am not God or a god. I am human and navigating a sex negative religious culture, your expectations of me while trying to deal with my own shit. The fact that I go out on dates and have sex has nothing to do with your personal relationship with God. I'm human, too. I am like many of the people God called upon in the Bible to do His work. I am an imperfect servant who is living under the grace of God, and I strive daily to be a better person. I confess, I struggle with lusting in the heart. Some "true believers" will say I have fallen and point to the book as personal proof of the need to oppose seminarians who date, have sex and still believe they are called to work for God.

My greatest fear is growing old alone. Dying alone and never experiencing what it is like to find "the one." Accepting that I may be alone for the rest of my life because I am becoming a minister is gut-wrenching. I don't want to be the cat lady or a spinster. There's a lot of shit that comes with becoming a minister that no one talks about. It's going to take someone special to be by my side.

I hope my confession has provided you with a little insight on the struggles of some seminarians, not all. I published these stories because I hope the insight into the dating lives of some seminarians will help you clear your mind of all your expectations about clergy and what they are, but most importantly who you think they should be in their private lives. Clear your mind of definitions that say real seminarians do not yearn for love, sex, or companionship. I hope you can clear your mind of any judgment that says what someone who is on the path to becoming clergy "should" be or that it "should be easier for seminarians to find love because they are on a spiritual path."

I had lots of sex in the seminary. I'm not proud of my behavior. I made many mistakes that I now regret. I want to find love, too.

As for "no sex"—don't you believe it. At some point in their lives, all seminarians get laid.


*End*

# About the Author

Ameila Strang is a seminary graduate who lives in Saint Paul, Minnesota. She is also the mother of two children.